Impressum
Verlag: BABADADA GmbH, Nedderfeld 112 , 22529 Hamburg
Geschäftsführer / Verlagsleitung: Harald Hof
Druck: Books on Demand GmbH, In de Tarpen 42, 22848 Norderstedt

Imprint
Publisher: BABADADA GmbH, Nedderfeld 112 , 22529 Hamburg, Germany
Managing Director / Publishing direction: Harald Hof
Print: Books on Demand GmbH, In de Tarpen 42, 22848 Norderstedt

school
school

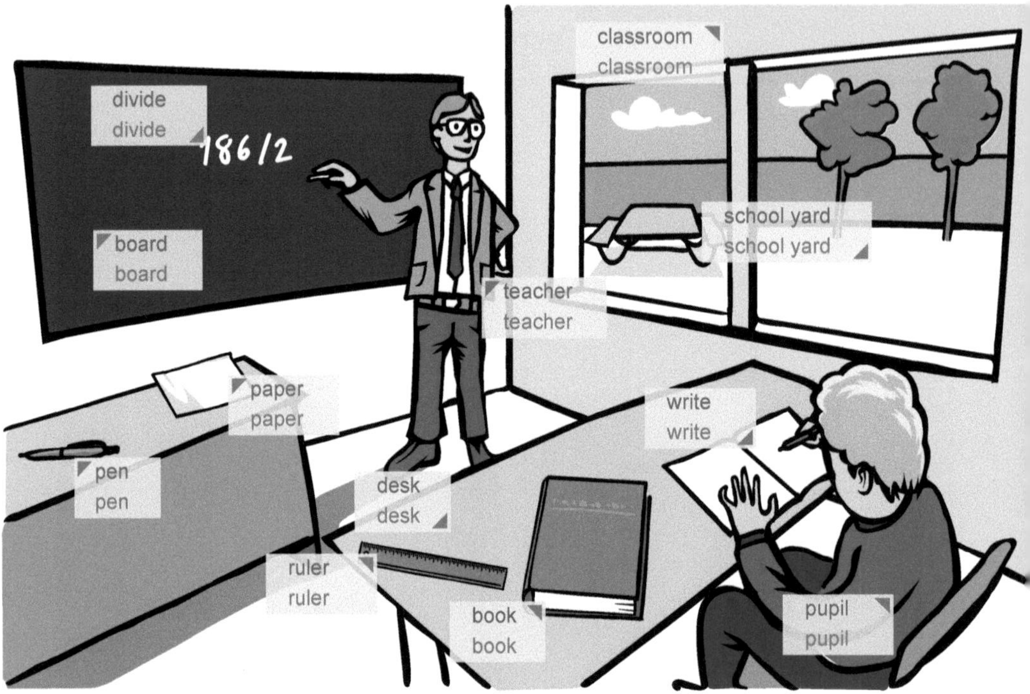
classroom
classroom
divide
divide
186/2
board
board
school yard
school yard
teacher
teacher
paper
paper
write
write
pen
pen
desk
desk
ruler
ruler
book
book
pupil
pupil

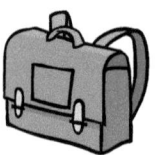

satchel
satchel

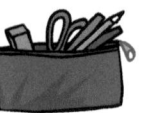

pencil case
pencil case

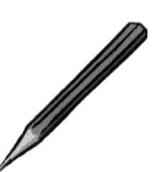

pencil
pencil

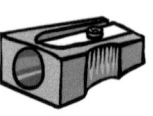

pencil sharpener
pencil sharpener

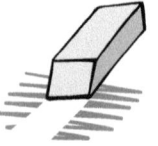

rubber
rubber

drawing pad
drawing pad

drawing

drawing

paintbrush

paintbrush

paint box

paint box

scissors

scissors

glue

glue

exercise book

exercise book

homework

homework

number

number

add

add

subtract

subtract

multiply

multiply

calculate

calculate

letter

letter

alphabet

alphabet

word

word

text

text

read

read

chalk

chalk

lesson

lesson

register

register

exam

examination

certificate

certificate

school uniform

school uniform

education

education

encyclopedia

encyclopedia

university

university

microscope

microscope

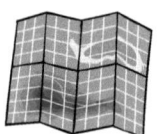

map

map

waste-paper basket

waste-paper basket

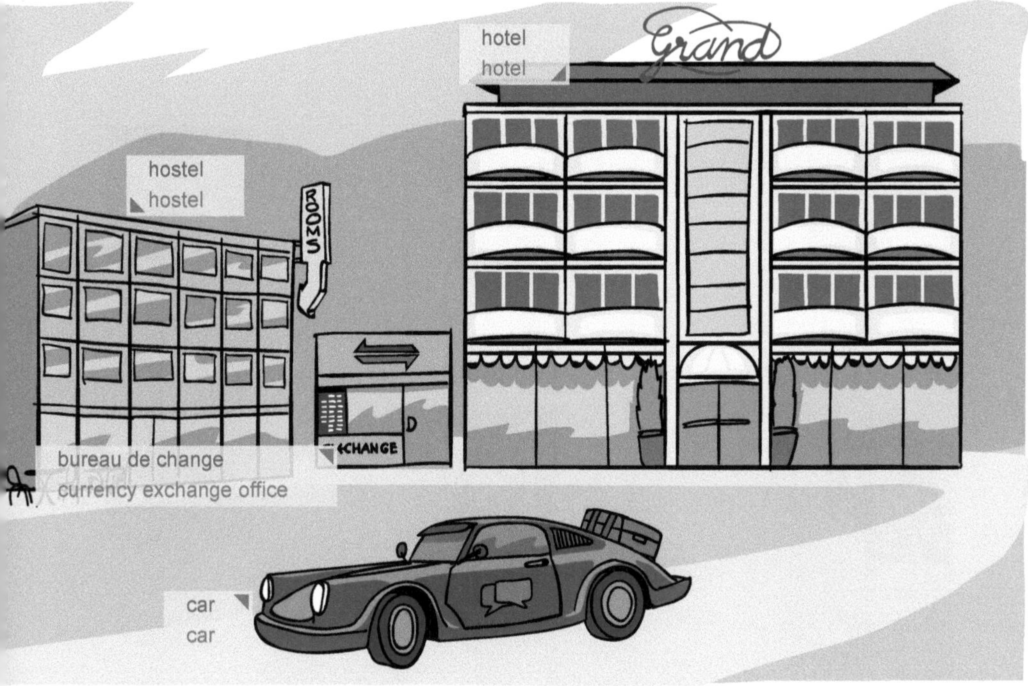

hotel
hotel
Grand
hostel
hostel
ROOMS
EXCHANGE
bureau de change
currency exchange office
car
car

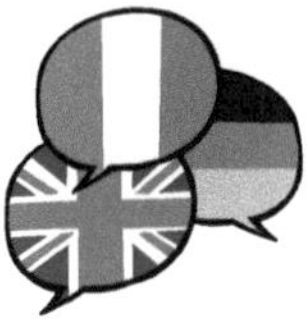

language

language

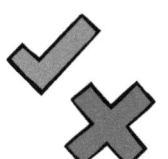

yes / no

yes / no

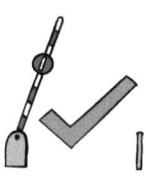

Okay

Okay

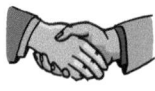

hello

hello

translator

translator

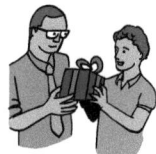

Thank you

Thank you

how much is…?

how much is…?

I do not understand

I don´t get it

problem

problem

Good evening!

Good evening!

Good morning!

Good morning!

Good night!

Good night!

bye bye

goodbye

direction

direction

luggage

luggage

bag

bag

backpack

backpack

guest

guest

room

room

sleeping bag

sleeping bag

tent

tent

travel - travel

tourist information
tourist information

beach
beach

credit card
credit card

breakfast
breakfast

lunch
lunch

dinner
dinner

ticket
Ticket

lift
elevator

stamp
stamp

border
border

customs
customs

embassy
embassy

visa
visa

passport
passport

transport

transport

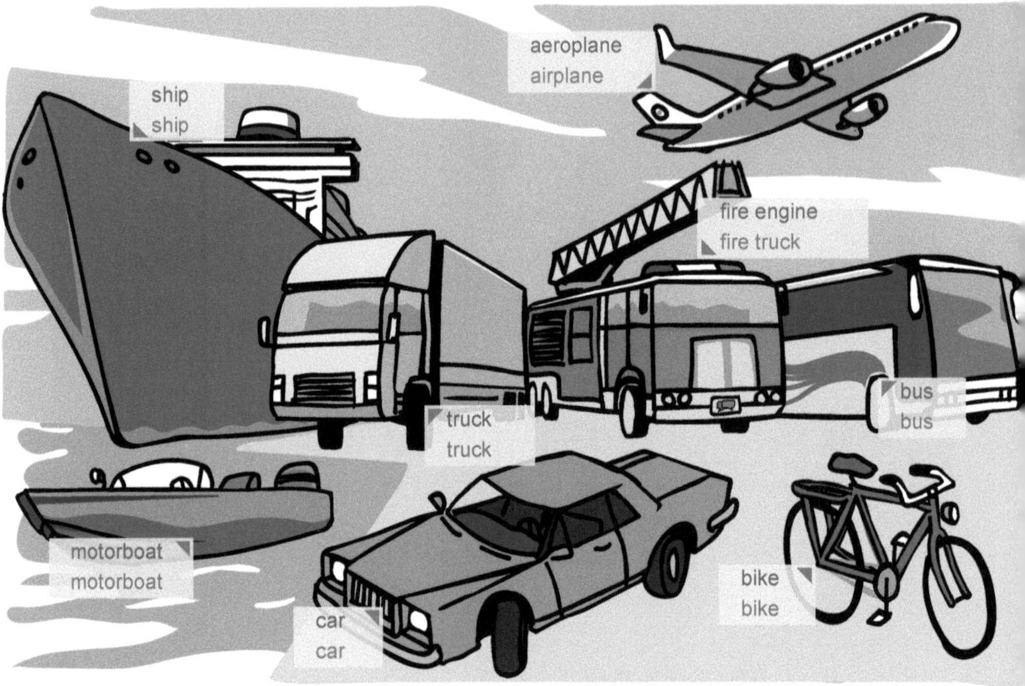
aeroplane
airplane
ship
ship
fire engine
fire truck
bus
bus
truck
truck
motorboat
motorboat
bike
bike
car
car

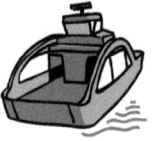

ferry
ferry

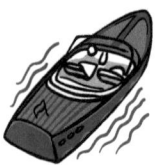

boat
boat

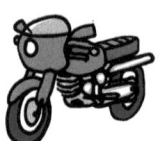

motorbike
motorbike

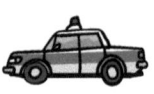

police car
police car

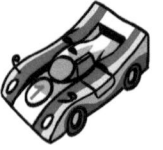

racing car
racing car

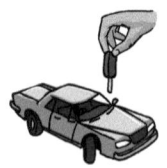

rental car
rental car

car sharing
car sharing

breakdown truck
tow truck

refuse truck
garbage truck

motor
engine

fuel
fuel

petrol station
fuel station

traffic sign
traffic sign

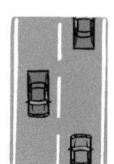

traffic
traffic

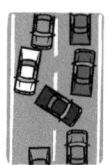

traffic jam
traffic jam

car park
parking lot

train station
train station

tracks
tracks

train
train

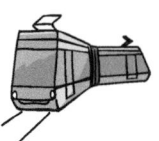

tram
tram

carriage
wagon

helicopter

helicopter

airport

airport

tower

tower

passenger

passenger

container

container

carton

carton

cart

cart

basket

basket

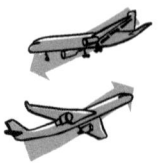

take off / land

take off / land

city

city

village

village

city centre

city center

house

house

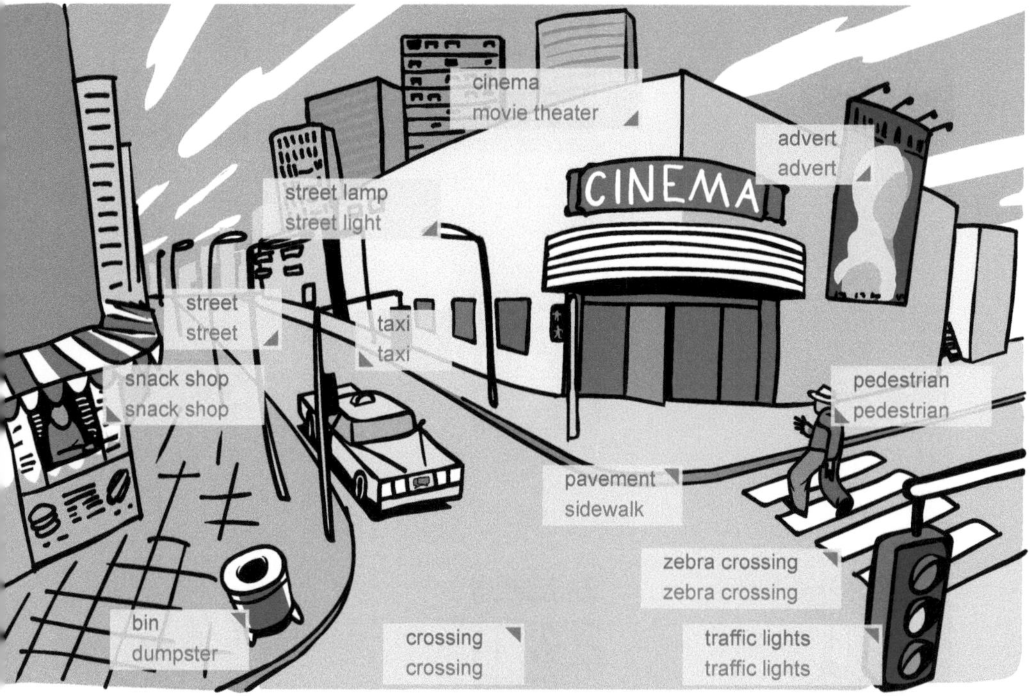

cinema
movie theater

advert
advert

street lamp
street light

CINEMA

street
street

taxi
taxi

pedestrian
pedestrian

snack shop
snack shop

pavement
sidewalk

zebra crossing
zebra crossing

bin
dumpster

crossing
crossing

traffic lights
traffic lights

hut
hut

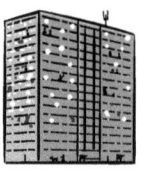

flat
apartment

train station
train station

town hall
city hall

museum
museum

school
school

university

university

bank

bank

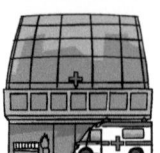

hospital

hospital

hotel

hotel

pharmacy

pharmacy

office

office

book shop

book shop

shop

shop

florist's

flower shop

supermarket

supermarket

market

market

department store

department store

fishmonger's

fishmonger's shop

shopping centre

mall

harbour

harbor

park

park

bench

bench

bridge

bridge

stairs

stairs

underground

subway

tunnel

tunnel

bus stop

bus stop

bar

bar

restaurant

restaurant

postbox

postbox

street sign

street sign

parking meter

parking meter

zoo

zoo

swimming pool

swimming pool

mosque

mosque

farm

farm

pollution

pollution

graveyard

cemetery

church

church

playground

playground

temple

temple

landscape

landscape

signpost
signpost

way
path

meadow
meadow

stone
stone

tree
tree

hiker
hiker

river
river

grass
grass

flower
flower

valley

valley

hill

hill

lake

lake

forest

forest

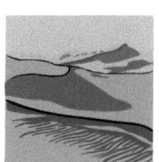

desert

desert

volcano

volcano

castle

castle

rainbow

rainbow

mushroom

mushroom

palm tree

palm tree

mosquito

mosquito

fly

fly

ant

ant

bee

bee

spider

spider

beetle

beetle

frog

frog

squirrel

squirrel

hedgehog

hedgehog

hare

hare

owl

owl

bird

bird

swan

swan

boar

boar

deer

deer

moose

moose

dam

dam

wind turbine

wind turbine

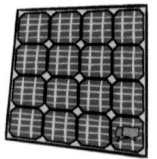

solar panel

solar panel

climate

climate

landscape - landscape

restaurant
restaurant

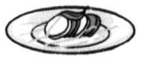

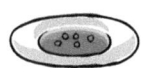

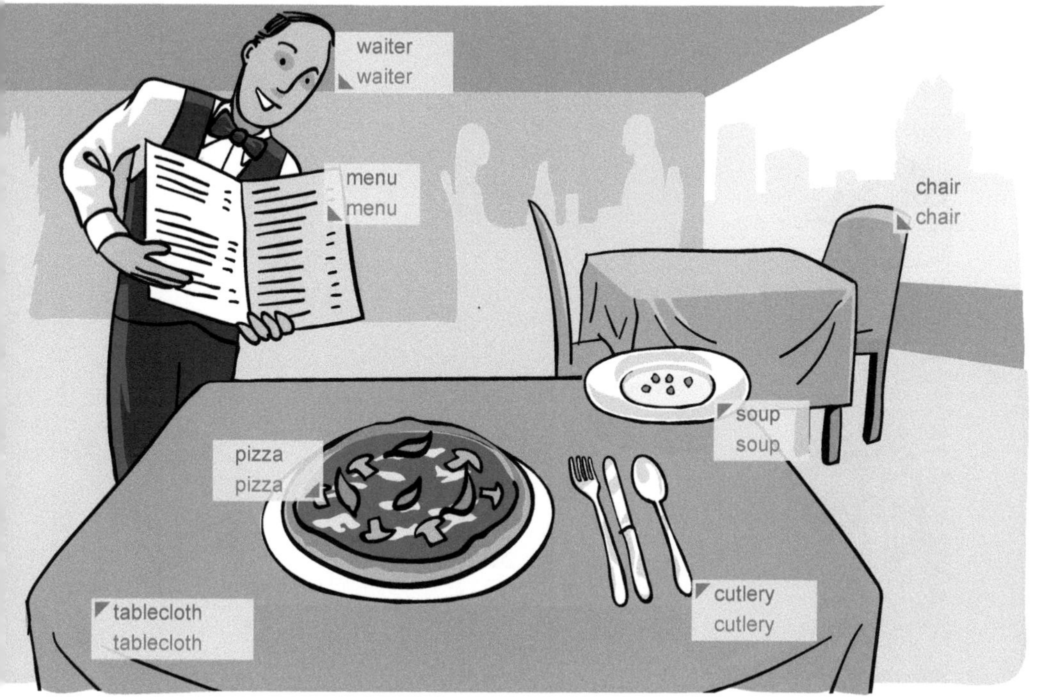
waiter
waiter
menu
menu
chair
chair
soup
soup
pizza
pizza
tablecloth
tablecloth
cutlery
cutlery

starter
starter

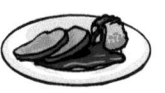

main course
main course

dessert
dessert

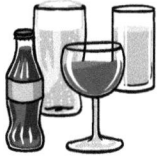

drinks
drinks

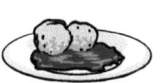

food
food

bottle
bottle

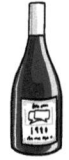

fast food

fast food

street food

street food

teapot

teapot

sugar bowl

sugar bowl

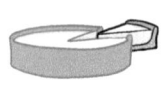

portion

portion

espresso machine

espresso machine

high chair

high chair

bill

bill

tray

tray

knife

knife

fork

fork

spoon

spoon

teaspoon

teaspoon

serviette

serviette

glass

glass

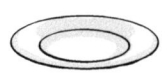

plate

plate

soup plate

soup plate

saucer

saucer

sauce

sauce

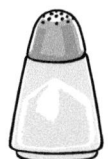

salt pot

salt shaker

pepper mill

pepper mill

vinegar

vinegar

oil

oil

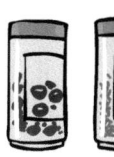

spices

spices

ketchup

ketchup

mustard

mustard

mayonnaise

mayonnaise

supermarket
supermarket

special offer
special offer
FOR
customer
customer
dairy
dairy products
fruit
fruit
trolley
shopping cart

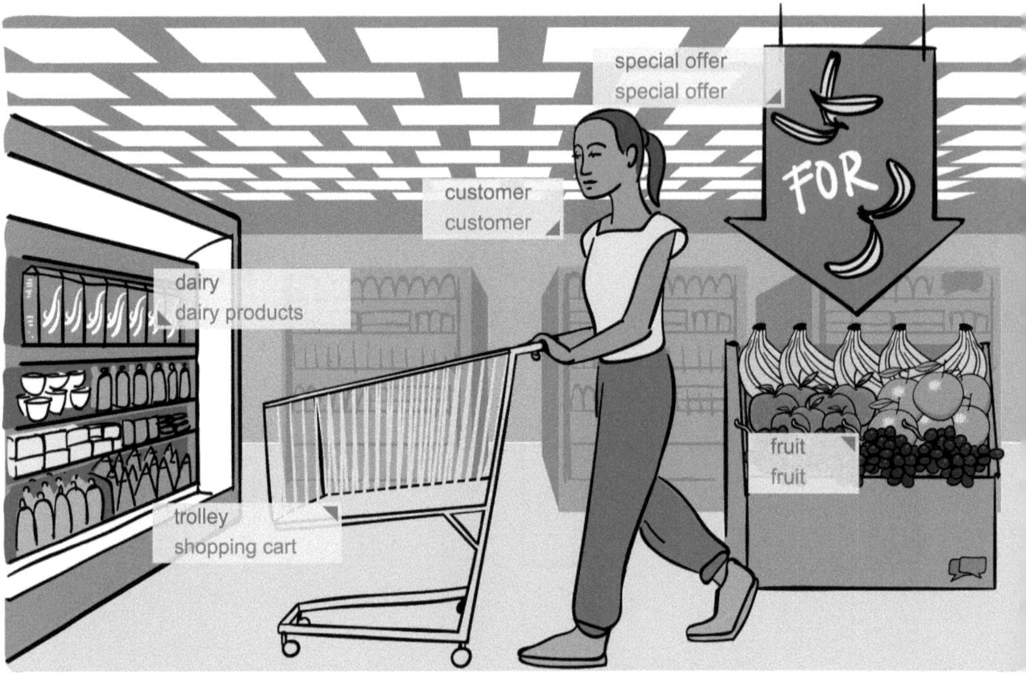

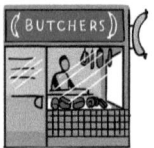

BUTCHERS

butcher´s

butcher's shop

BAKERY

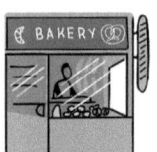

baker´s

bakery

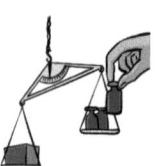

weigh

weigh

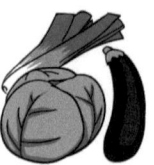

vegetables

vegetables

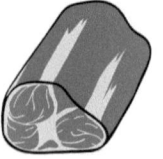

meat

meat

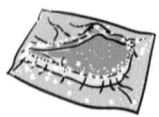

frozen food

frozen food

cold meat

cold cuts

tinned food

canned food

washing powder

detergent

sweets

candy

household products

household products

cleaning products

cleaning products

salesperson

sales representative

till

cash register

cashier

cashier

shopping list

shopping list

opening hours

opening hours

wallet

wallet

credit card

credit card

bag

bag

plastic bag

plastic bag

water

water

juice

juice

milk

milk

coke

coke

wine

wine

beer

beer

alcohol

alcohol

cocoa

cocoa

tea

tea

coffee

coffee

espresso

espresso

cappuccino

cappuccino

banana

banana

apple

apple

orange

orange

melon

melon

lemon

lemon

carrot

carrot

garlic

garlic

bamboo

bamboo

onion

onion

mushroom

mushroom

nuts

nuts

noodles

noodles

spaghetti

spaghetti

rice

rice

salad

salad

chips

fries

fried potatoes

fried potatoes

pizza

pizza

hamburger

hamburger

sandwich

sandwich

cutlet

escalope

ham

ham

salami

salami

sausage

sausage

chicken

chicken

roast

roast

fish

fish

porridge oats

porridge oats

muesli

muesli

cornflakes

cornflakes

flour

flour

croissant

croissant

bread roll

bread roll

bread

bread

toast

toast

biscuits

cookies

butter

butter

curd

curd

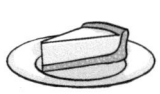

cake

cake

egg

egg

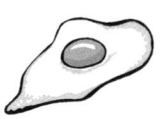

fried egg

fried egg

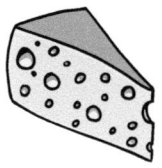

cheese

cheese

ice cream

ice cream

sugar

sugar

honey

honey

jam

jelly

chocolate spread

nougat cream

curry

curry

farm

farm

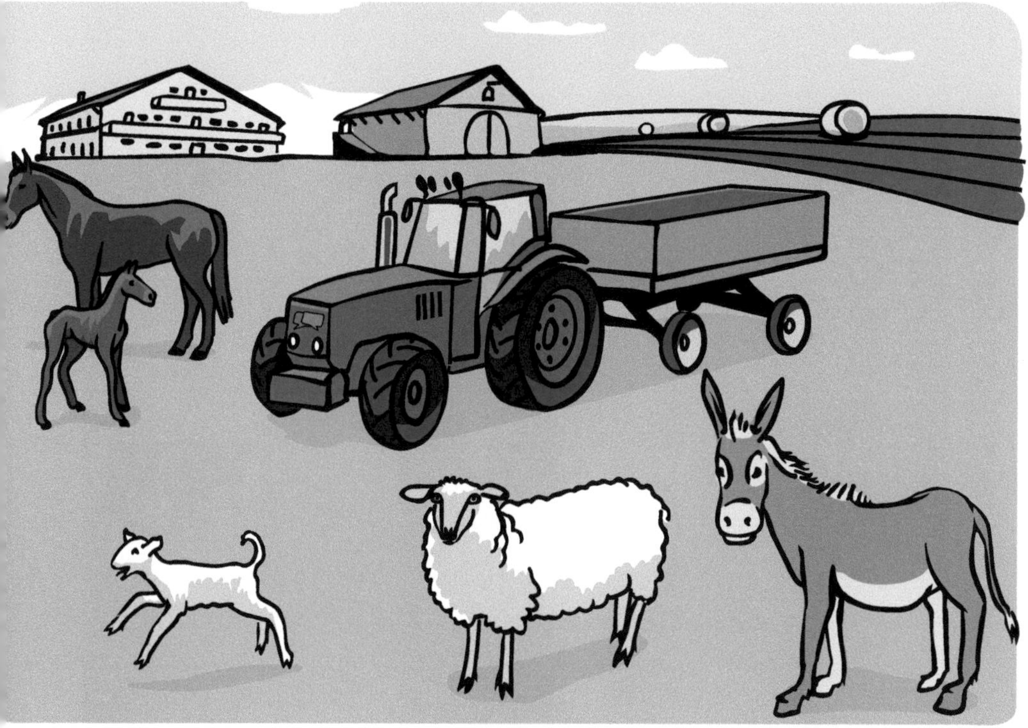

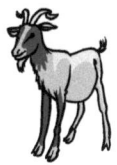

goat

goat

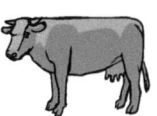

cow

cow

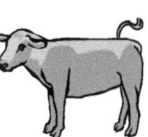

calf

calf

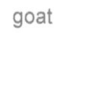

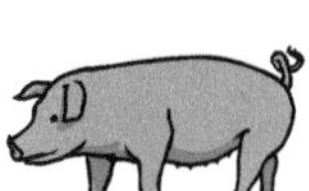

pig

pig

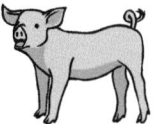

piglet

piglet

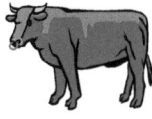

bull

bull

goose

goose

duck

duck

chick

chick

hen

hen

cock

cockerel

rat

rat

cat

cat

mouse

mouse

ox

ox

dog

dog

doghouse

dog house

garden hose

garden hose

watering can

watering can

scythe

scythe

plough

plow

sickle

sickle

hoe

hoe

pitchfork

pitchfork

axe

axe

wheelbarrow

pushcart

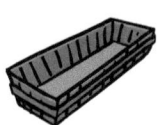

trough

trough

milk can

milk can

sack

sack

fence

fence

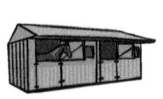

stable

stable

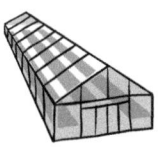

greenhouse

greenhouse

soil

soil

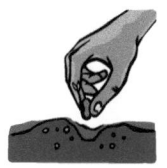

seed

seed

fertilizer

fertilizer

combine harvester

combine harvester

harvest

harvest

harvest

harvest

yams

yams

wheat

wheat

soy

soya

potato

potato

corn

corn

rapeseed

rapeseed

fruit tree

fruit tree

cassava

manioc

cereals

grain

living room living room	bathroom bathroom	kitchen kitchen

living room
living room

bathroom
bathroom

kitchen
kitchen

bedroom
bedroom

child's room
kids room

dining room
dining room

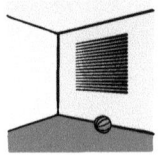

floor

floor

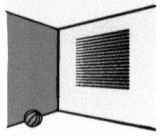

wall

wall

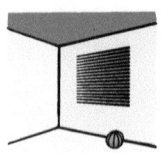

ceiling

ceiling

cellar

cellar

sauna

sauna

balcony

balcony

terrace

terrace

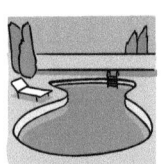

pool

pool

lawn mower

lawn mower

sheet

sheet

bedspread

bedspread

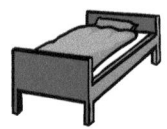

bed

bed

broom

broom

bucket

bucket

switch

switch

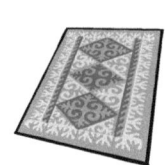

living room

living room

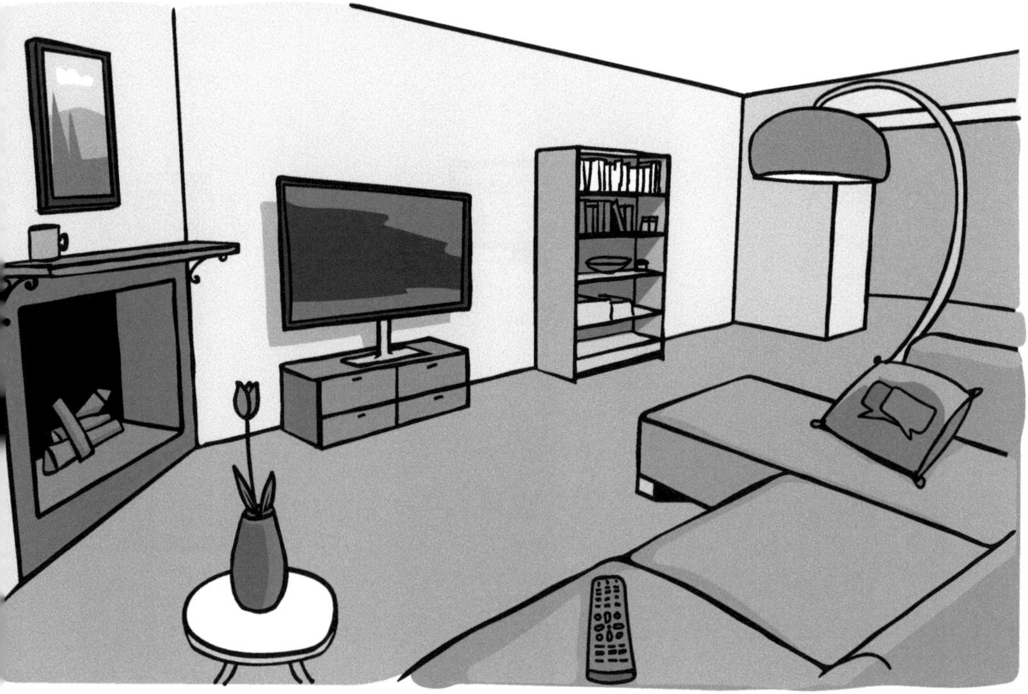

carpet
carpet

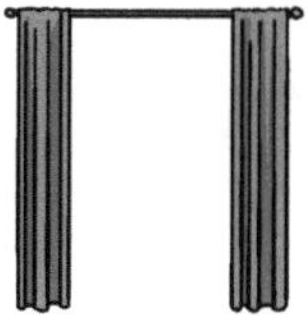

curtain
drape

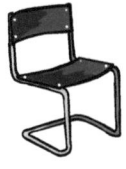

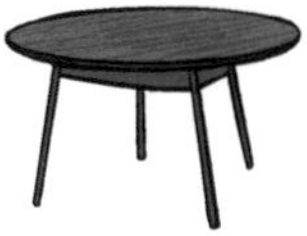

table
table

chair
chair

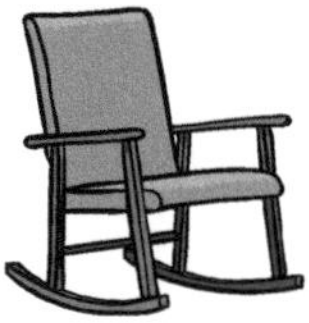

rocking chair
rocking chair

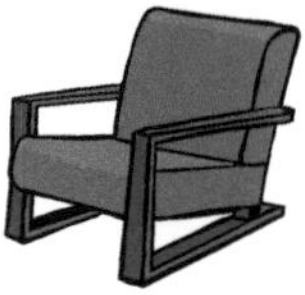

armchair
armchair

book
book

blanket
blanket

decoration
decoration

firewood
firewood

film
film

hi-fi equipment
stereo system

key
key

newspaper
newspaper

painting
painting

poster
poster

radio
radio

notepad
notebook

hoover
vacuum cleaner

cactus
cactus

candle
candle

kitchen
kitchen

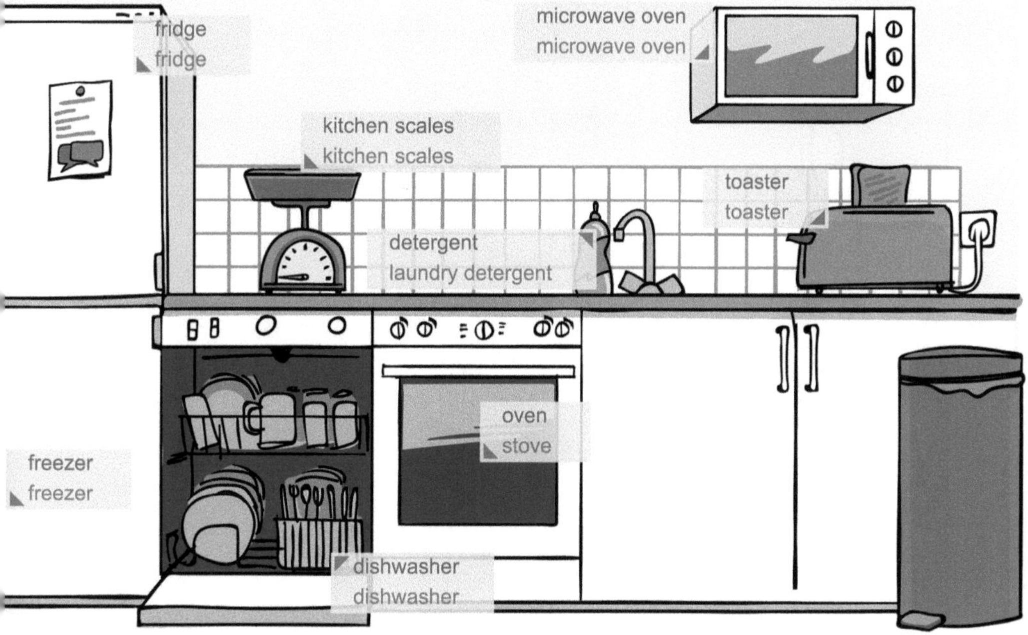
fridge
fridge
microwave oven
microwave oven
kitchen scales
kitchen scales
toaster
toaster
detergent
laundry detergent
oven
stove
freezer
freezer
dishwasher
dishwasher

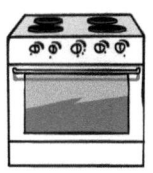

cooker

cooker

pot

pot

cast-iron pot

cast-iron pot

wok / kadai

wok / kadai

pan

pan

kettle

kettle

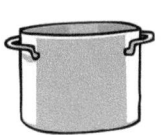

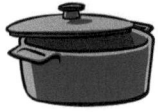

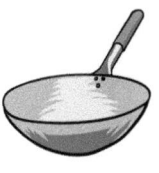

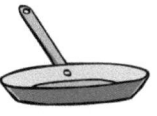

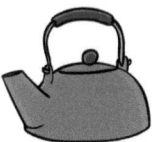

steamer

steamer

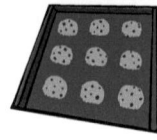

baking tray

baking tray

crockery

crockery

mug

mug

bowl

bowl

chopsticks

chopsticks

ladle

ladle

spatula

spatula

whisk

whisk

strainer

strainer

sieve

sieve

grater

grater

mortar

mortar

barbecue

barbecue

open fire

fireplace

chopping board

chopping board

rolling pin

rolling pin

corkscrew

corkscrew

can

can

can opener

can opener

pot holder

oven cloth

sink

sink

brush

brush

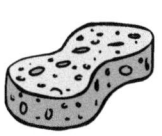

sponge

sponge

blender

blender

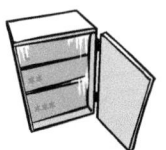

deep freezer

deep freezer

baby bottle

baby bottle

tap

tap

kitchen - kitchen

bathroom
bathroom

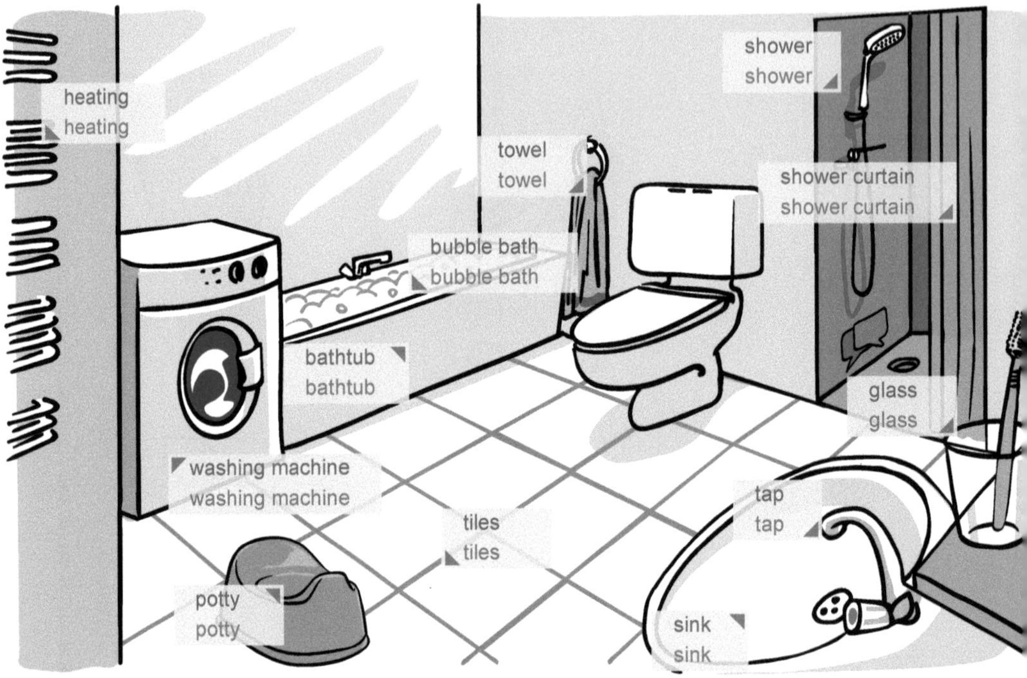
heating
heating
towel
towel
shower
shower
shower curtain
shower curtain
bubble bath
bubble bath
bathtub
bathtub
glass
glass
washing machine
washing machine
tap
tap
tiles
tiles
potty
potty
sink
sink

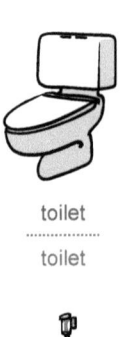

toilet
toilet

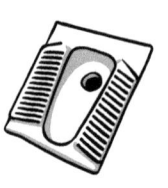

squat toilet
squat toilet

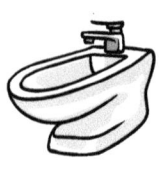

bidet
bidet

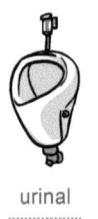

urinal
urinal

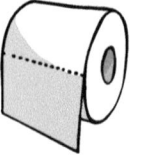

toilet paper
toilet paper

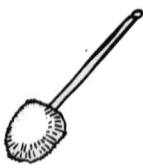

toilet brush
toilet brush

toothbrush

toothbrush

toothpaste

toothpaste

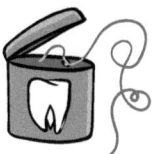

dental floss

dental floss

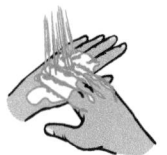

wash

wash

handheld shower

hand shower

douche

douche

basin

basin

back brush

back brush

soap

soap

shower gel

shower gel

shampoo

shampoo

flannel

flannel

drain

drain

cream

creme

deodorant

deodorant

mirror

mirror

hand mirror

hand mirror

razor

razor

shaving foam

shaving foam

aftershave

aftershave

comb

comb

brush

brush

hair dryer

hair-dryer

hairspray

hairspray

makeup

makeup

lipstick

lipstick

nail varnish

nail varnish

cotton wool

cotton wool

nail scissors

nail scissors

perfume

perfume

washbag

washbag

stool

stool

weighing scale

weighing scales

bathrobe

bathrobe

rubber gloves

rubber gloves

tampon

tampon

sanitary towel

sanitary towel

chemical toilet

chemical toilet

child's room

kids room

alarm clock
alarm clock
cuddly toy
cuddly toy
toy car
toy car
rattle
rattle
doll's house
doll's house
present
present

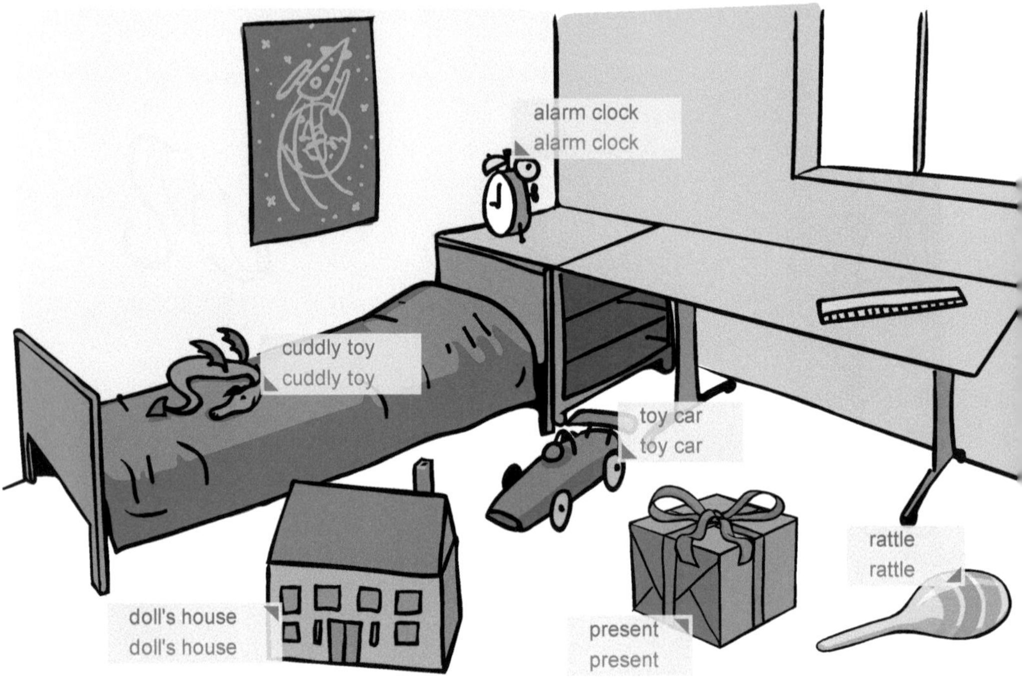

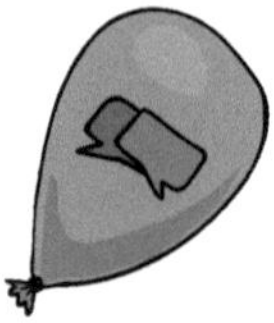

balloon

balloon

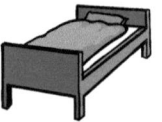

bed

bed

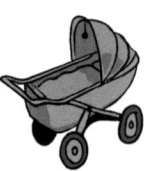

pram

stroller

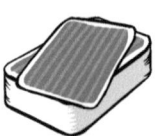

deck of cards

deck of cards

jigsaw

jigsaw

SUPER MEGA

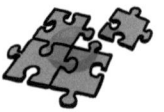

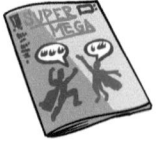

comic

comic

lego bricks
....
lego bricks

building blocks
....
toy blocks

action figure
....
action figure

babygrow
....
romper suit

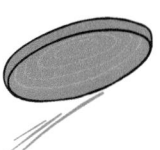

frisbee
....
frisbee

mobile
....
mobile

board game
....
board game

dice
....
dice

model train set
....
model train set

dummy
....
pacifier

party
....
party

picture book
....
picture book

ball
....
ball

doll
....
doll

play
....
play

sandpit

sandpit

swing

swing

toys

toys

video game console

video game console

tricycle

tricycle

teddy bear

teddy bear

wardrobe

wardrobe

clothing

clothing

socks

socks

stockings

stockings

tights

tights

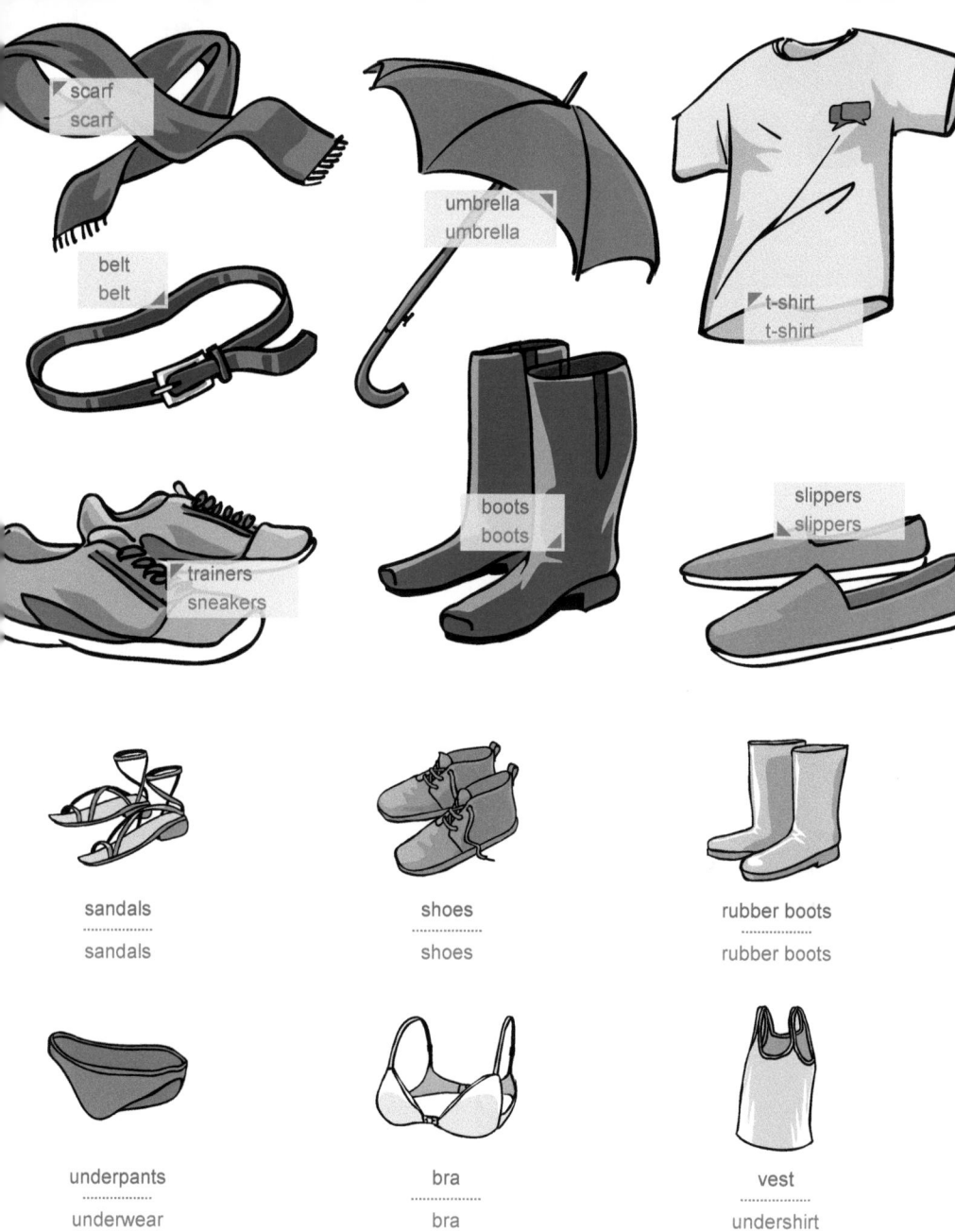

scarf
scarf

belt
belt

umbrella
umbrella

t-shirt
t-shirt

trainers
sneakers

boots
boots

slippers
slippers

sandals
....
sandals

shoes
....
shoes

rubber boots
....
rubber boots

underpants
....
underwear

bra
....
bra

vest
....
undershirt

body
body

trousers
pants

jeans
jeans

skirt
skirt

blouse
blouse

shirt
shirt

pullover
pullover

hoodie
sweater

blazer
blazer

jacket
jacket

coat
coat

raincoat
raincoat

costume
costume

dress
dress

wedding dress
wedding dress

suit

suit

nightgown

nightgown

pyjamas

pajamas

sari

sari

headscarf

headscarf

turban

turban

burqa

burka

kaftan

kaftan

abaya

abaya

swimsuit

swimsuit

trunks

trunks

shorts

shorts

tracksuit

tracksuit

apron

apron

gloves

gloves

button
button

glasses
glasses

bracelet
bracelet

necklace
necklace

ring
ring

earring
earring

cap
cap

coat hanger
coat hanger

hat
hat

tie
tie

zip
zip

helmet
helmet

braces
braces

school uniform
school uniform

uniform
uniform

clothing - clothing

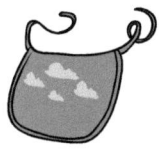

bib

bib

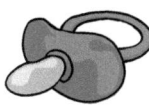

dummy

pacifier

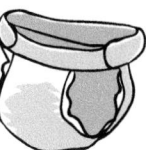

nappy

diaper

office

office

server
server
filing cabinet
filing cabinet
paper
paper
printer
printer
monitor
monitor
mouse
mouse
desk
desk
folder
folder
keyboard
keyboard
waste-paper basket
waste-paper basket
chair
chair
computer
computer

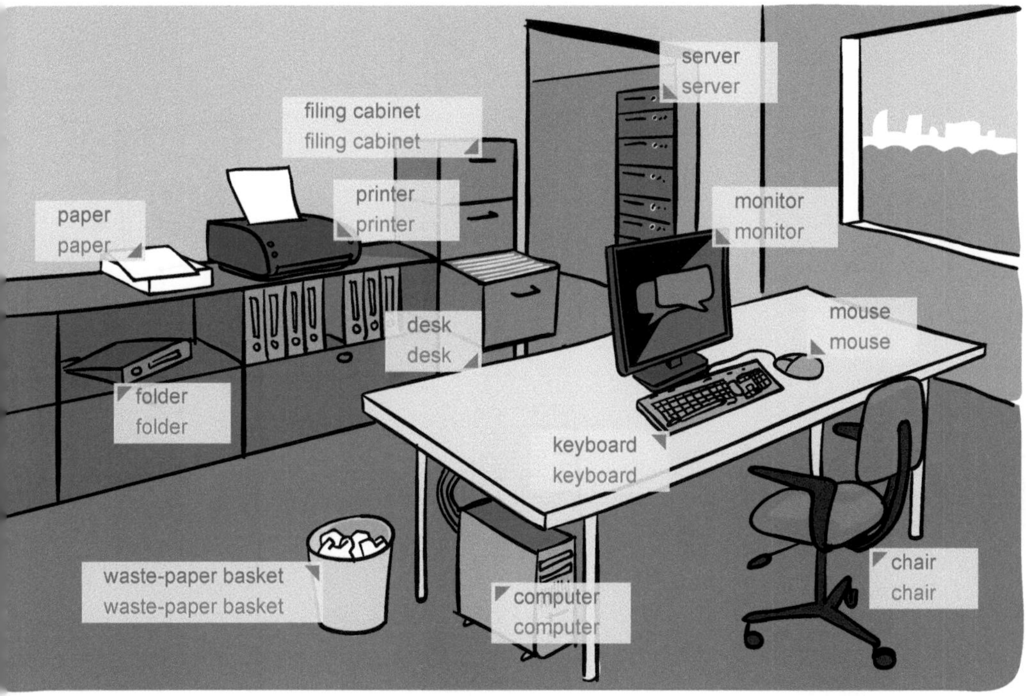

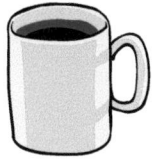

coffee mug

coffee mug

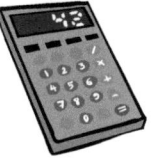

calculator

calculator

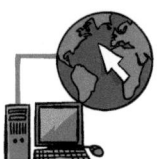

internet

internet

laptop
laptop

letter
letter

message
message

mobile
cell phone

network
network

photocopier
photocopier

software
software

telephone
telephone

plug socket
plug socket

fax machine
fax machine

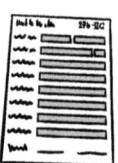

form
form

document
document

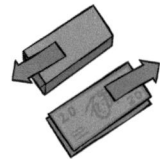

buy
buy

pay
pay

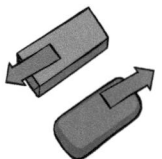

trade
trade

money
money

dollar
dollar

euro
euro

yen
yen

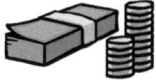

rouble
rouble

Swiss franc
Swiss franc

renminbi yuan
renminbi yuan

rupee
rupee

cashpoint
cash point

bureau de change
currency exchange office

gold
gold

silver
silver

oil
oil

energy
energy

price
price

contract
contract

tax
tax

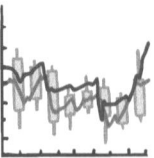

stock
stock

work
work

employee
employee

employer
employer

factory
factory

shop
shop

economy - economy

occupations
occupations

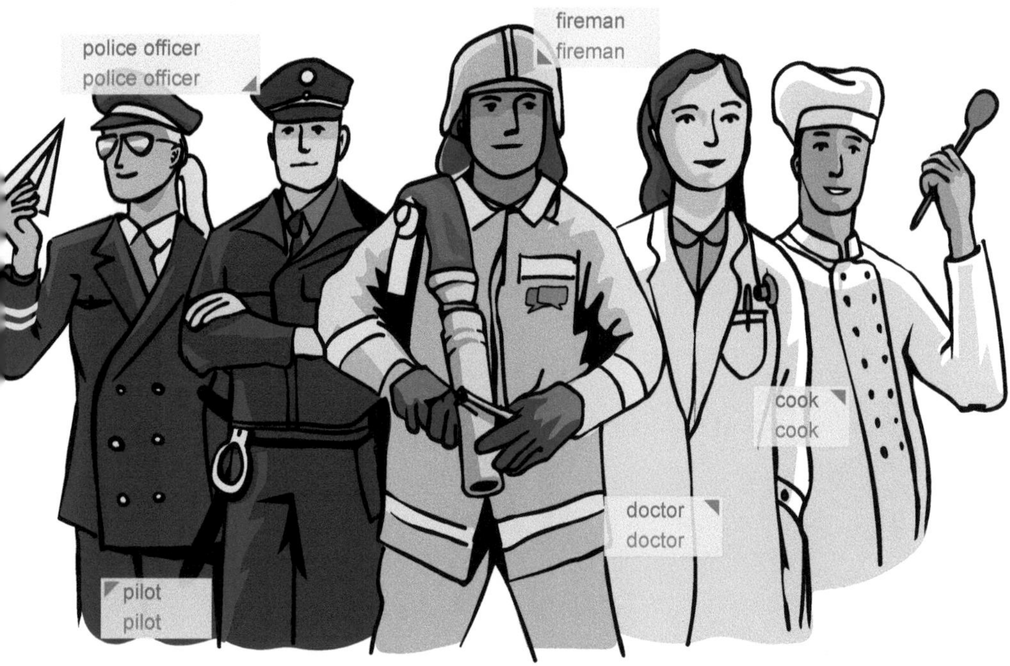
police officer
police officer
fireman
fireman
cook
cook
doctor
doctor
pilot
pilot

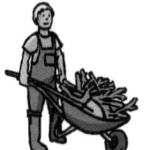

gardener

gardener

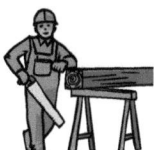

carpenter

carpenter

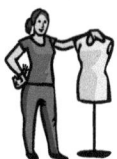

seamstress

seamstress

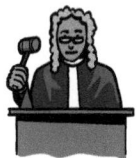

judge

judge

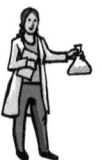

chemist

chemist

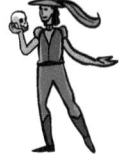

actor

actor

bus driver
bus driver

taxi driver
taxi driver

fisherman
fisherman

cleaning lady
cleaning lady

roofer
roofer

waiter
waiter

hunter
hunter

painter
painter

baker
baker

electrician
electrician

builder
builder

engineer
engineer

butcher
butcher

plumber
plumber

postman
postman

soldier

soldier

architect

architect

cashier

cashier

florist

florist

hairdresser

hairdresser

conductor

conductor

mechanic

mechanic

captain

captain

dentist

dentist

scientist

scientist

rabbi

rabbi

imam

imam

monk

monk

clergyman

pastor

occupations - occupations

tools

tools

hammer
hammer
pliers
pliers
screwdriver
screwdriver
spanner
wrench
torch
torch

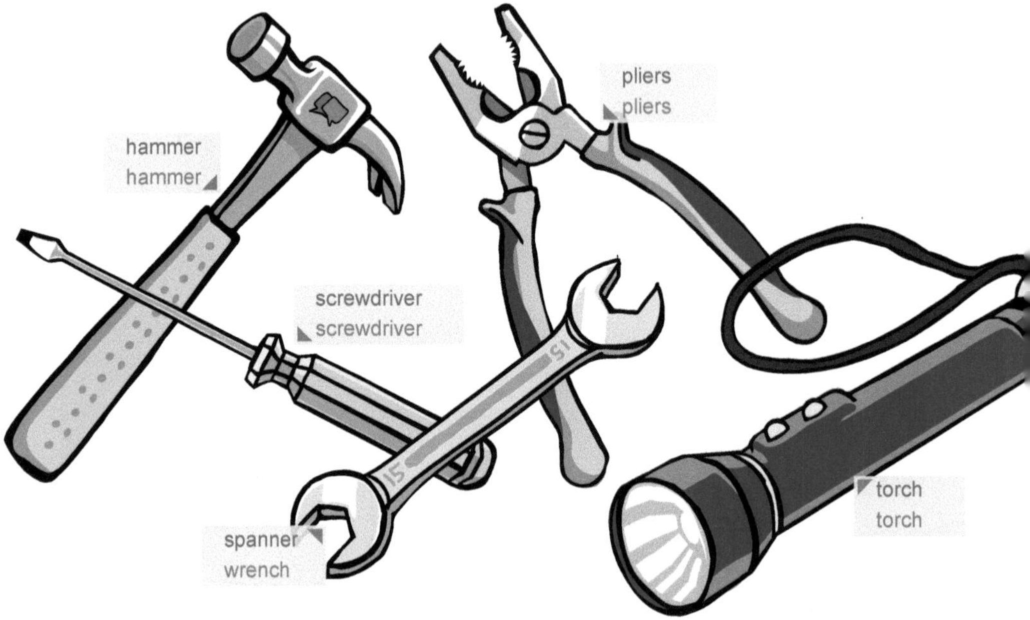

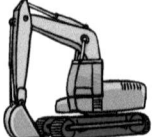

digger
excavator

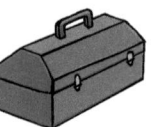

toolbox
toolbox

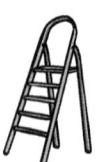

ladder
ladder

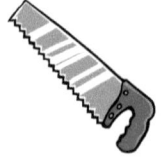

saw
saw

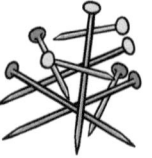

nails
nails

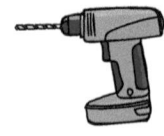

drill
drill

repair
repair

shovel
shovel

Damn!
Damn!

dustpan
dustpan

paint pot
paint can

screws
screws

musical instruments
musical instruments

drum kit
drum set

loudspeaker
loud speaker

guitar
guitar

double bass
double bass

trumpet
trumpet

piano

piano

violin

violin

bass

bass

timpani

timpani

drums

drums

keyboard

keyboard

saxophone

saxophone

flute

flute

microphone

microphone

entrance
entrance

tiger
tiger

cage
cage

zebra
zebra

animal feed
animal feed

panda
panda

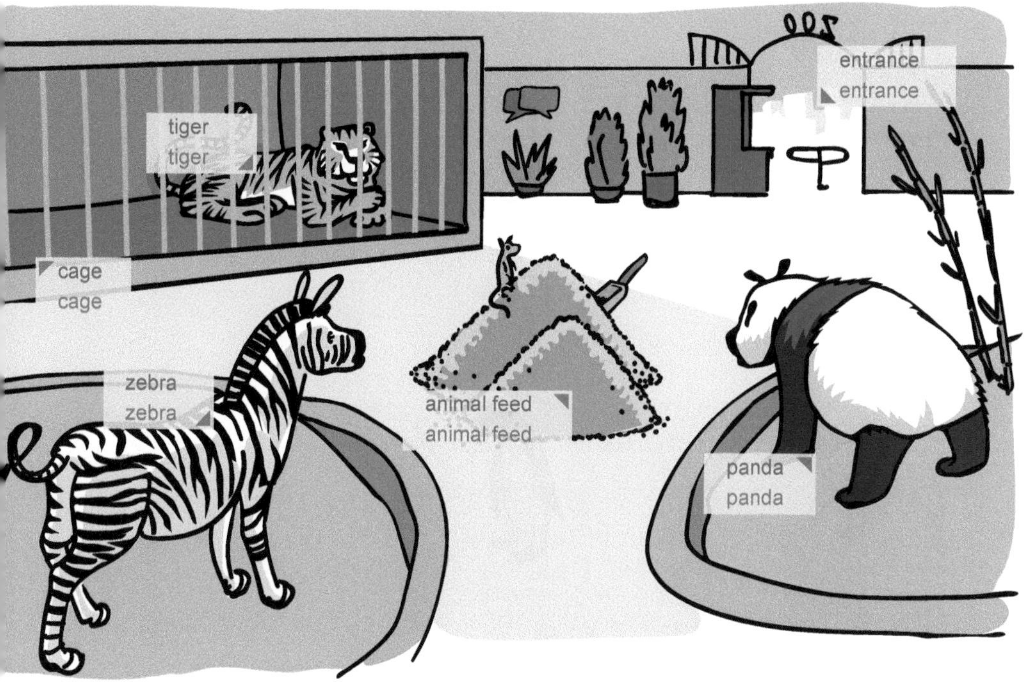

animals
animals

elephant
elephant

kangaroo
kangaroo

rhino
rhino

gorilla
gorilla

bear
bear

camel

camel

ostrich

ostrich

lion

lion

monkey

monkey

flamingo

flamingo

parrot

parrot

polar bear

polar bear

penguin

penguin

shark

shark

peacock

peacock

snake

snake

crocodile

crocodile

zookeeper

zookeeper

seal

seal

jaguar

jaguar

pony

pony

leopard

leopard

hippo

hippo

giraffe

giraffe

eagle

eagle

boar

boar

fish

fish

turtle

turtle

walrus

walrus

fox

fox

gazelle

gazelle

American football
American football

cycling
cycling

tennis
tennis

basketball
basketball

swimming
swimming

boxing
boxing

ice hockey
ice hockey

football
soccer

badminton
badminton

athletics
athletics

handball
handball

skiing
skiing

polo
polo

activities

jump
jump
sing
sing
hug
hug
laugh
laugh
walk
walk
dream
dream
pray
pray
kiss
kiss

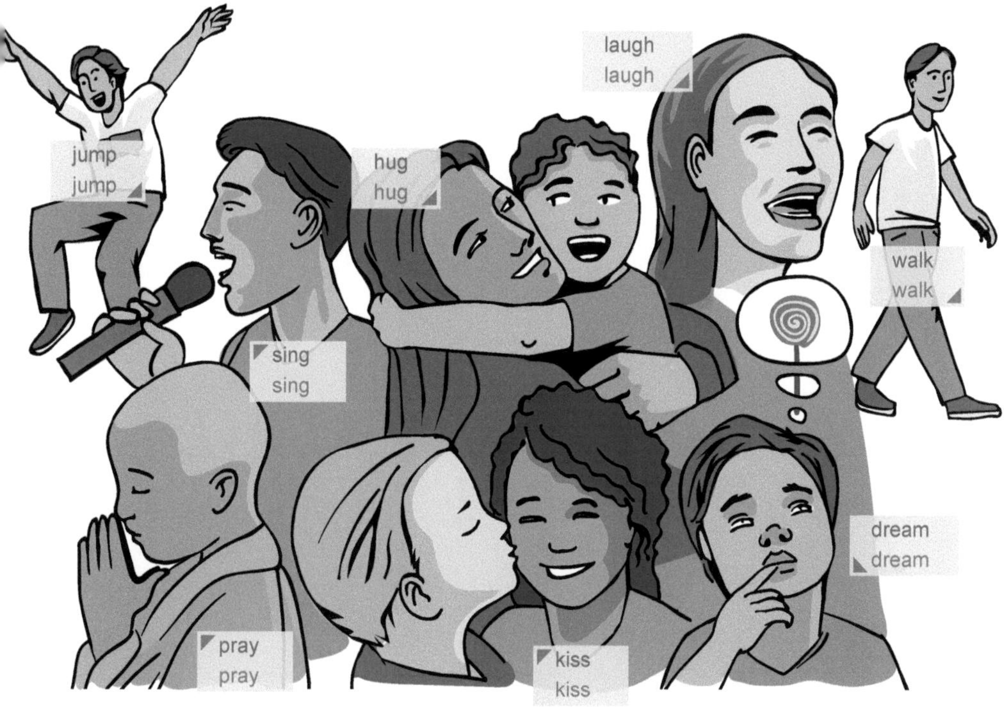

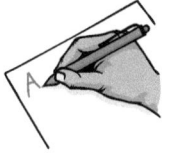

write
write

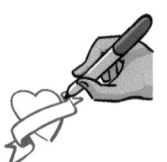

draw
draw

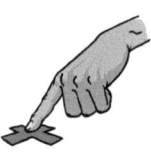

show
show

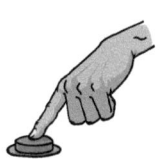

push
push

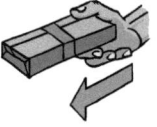

give
give

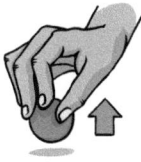

take
take

have

have

do

do

be

be

stand

stand

run

run

pull

pull

throw

throw

fall

fall

lie

lie

wait

wait

carry

carry

sit

sit

get dressed

get dressed

sleep

sleep

wake up

wake up

look at
look at

cry
cry

stroke
stroke

comb
comb

talk
talk

understand
understand

ask
ask

listen
listen

drink
drink

eat
eat

tidy up
tidy up

love
love

cook
cook

drive
drive

fly
fly

sail

sail

calculate

calculate

read

read

learn

learn

work

work

marry

marry

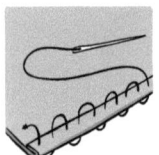

sew

sew

brush teeth

brush teeth

kill

kill

smoke

smoke

send

send

grandmother
grandmother

grandfather
grandfather

father
father

mother
mother

baby
baby

daughter
daughter

son
son

guest

guest

aunt

aunt

uncle

uncle

brother

brother

sister

sister

body

body

forehead
forehead
eye
eye
shoulder
shoulder
finger
finger
face
face
chin
chin
hand
hand
leg
leg
breast
breast
arm
arm

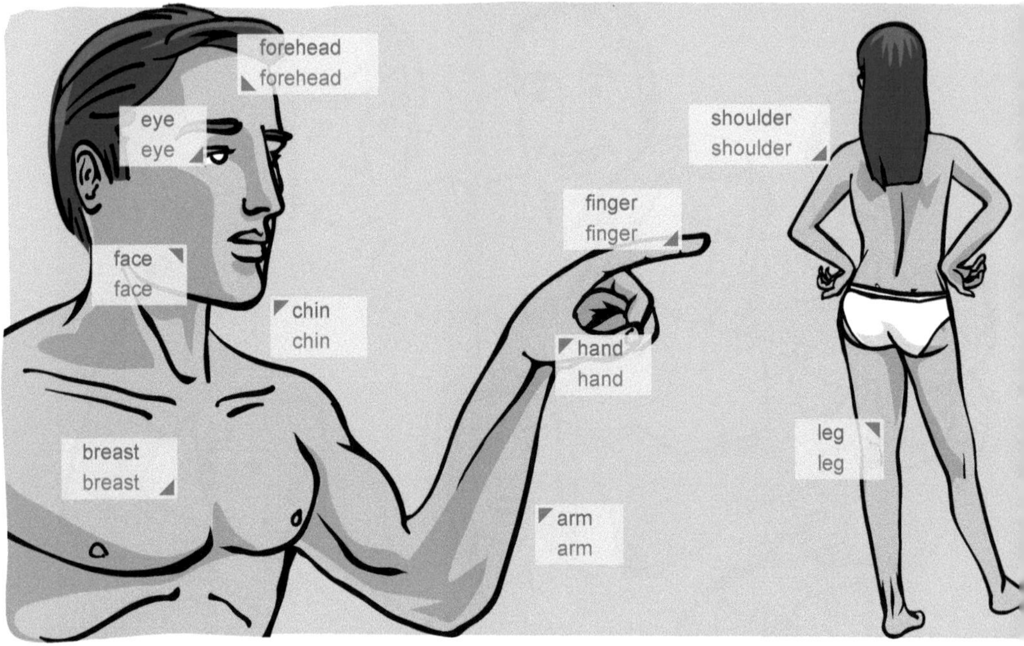

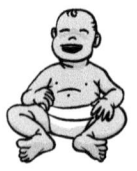

baby

baby

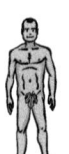

man

man

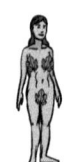

woman

woman

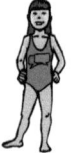

girl

girl

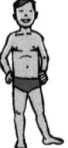

boy

boy

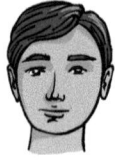

head

head

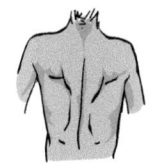

back

back

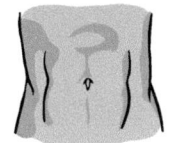

belly

belly

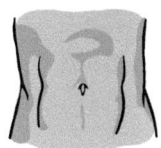

belly button

navel

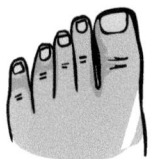

toe

toe

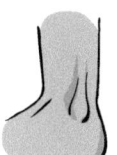

heel

heel

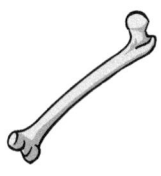

bone

bone

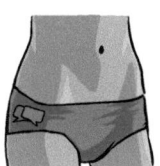

hip

hip

knee

knee

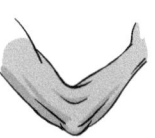

elbow

elbow

nose

nose

bottom

buttocks

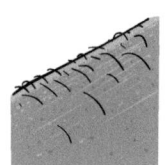

skin

skin

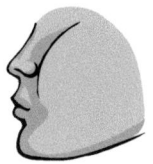

cheek

cheek

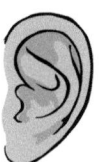

ear

ear

lip

lip

mouth

mouth

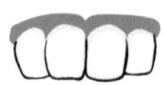

tooth

tooth

tongue

tongue

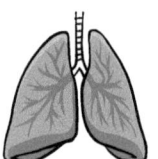

brain

brain

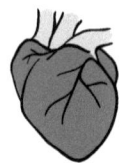

heart

heart

muscle

muscle

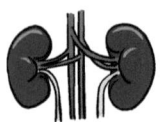

lung

lung

liver

liver

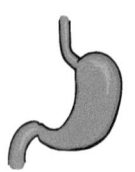

stomach

stomach

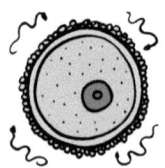

kidneys

kidneys

sex

sex

condom

condom

ovum

ovum

semen

semen

pregnancy

pregnancy

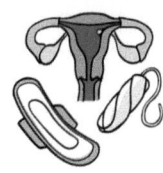

menstruation

menstruation

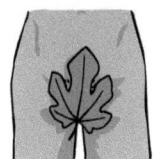

vagina

vagina

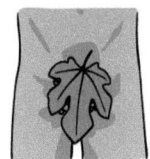

penis

penis

eyebrow

eyebrow

hair

hair

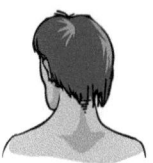

neck

neck

hospital

hospital

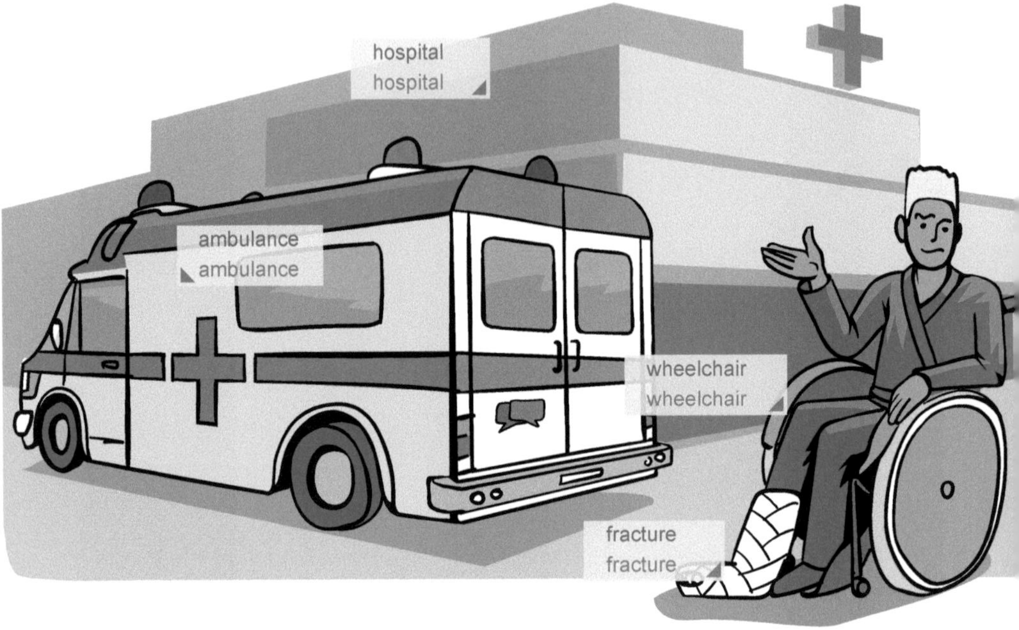
hospital
hospital
ambulance
ambulance
wheelchair
wheelchair
fracture
fracture

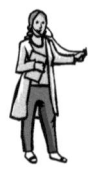

doctor

doctor

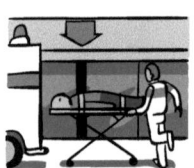

emergency room

emergency room

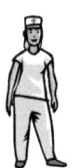

nurse

nurse

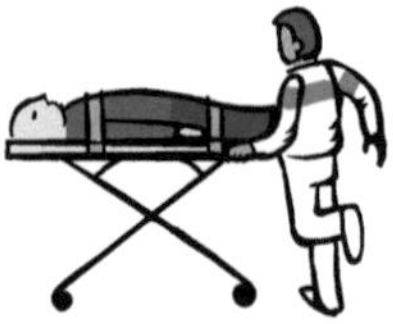

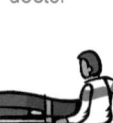

emergency

emergency

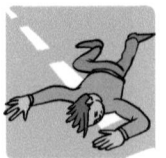

unconscious

unconscious

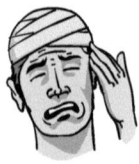

pain

pain

injury

injury

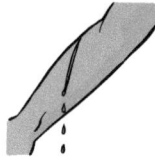

bleeding

bleeding

heart attack

heart attack

stroke

stroke

allergy

allergy

cough

cough

fever

fever

flu

flu

diarrhoea

diarrhea

headache

headache

cancer

cancer

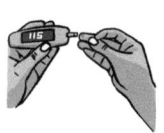

diabetes

diabetes

surgeon

surgeon

scalpel

scalpel

operation

operation

CT

CT

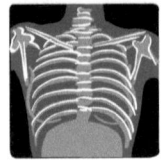

x-ray

x-ray

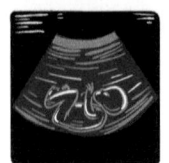

ultrasound

ultrasound

face mask

face mask

disease

disease

waiting room

waiting room

crutch

crutch

plaster

plaster

bandage

bandage

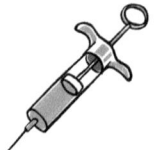

injection

injection

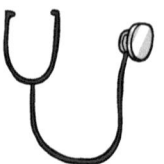

stethoscope

stethoscope

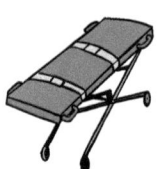

stretcher

stretcher

clinical thermometer

clinical thermometer

birth

birth

overweight

overweight

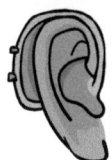

hearing aid

hearing aid

disinfectant

disinfectant

infection

infection

virus

virus

HIV / AIDS

HIV / AIDS

medicine

medicine

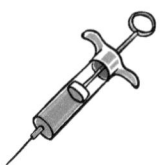

vaccination

vaccination

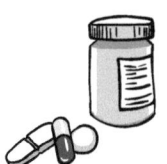

tablets

tablets

pill

pill

emergency call

emergency call

blood pressure monitor

blood pressure monitor

ill / healthy

ill / healthy

Help! Help!	 alarm alarm	 assault assault
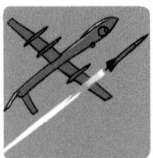 attack attack	 danger danger	 emergency exit emergency exit
Fire! Fire!	 fire extinguisher fire extinguisher	 accident accident
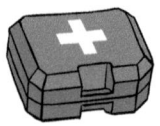 first-aid kit first-aid kit	 SOS SOS	 police police

Europe

Europe

North America

North America

South America

South America

Africa

Africa

Asia

Asia

Australia

Australia

Atlantic

Atlantic

Pacific

Pacific

Indian Ocean

Indian Ocean

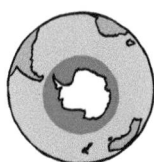

Antarctic Ocean

Antarctic Ocean

Arctic Ocean

Arctic Ocean

North Pole

North pole

South Pole
South pole

Antarctica
Antarctica

Earth
earth

land
land

sea
sea

island
island

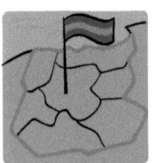

nation
nation

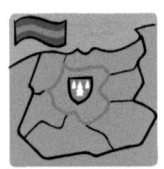

state
state

clock face

clock face

hour hand

hour hand

minute hand

minute hand

second hand

second hand

What time is it?

What time is it?

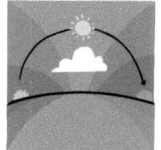

day

day

time

time

now

now

digital watch

digital watch

minute

minute

hour

hour

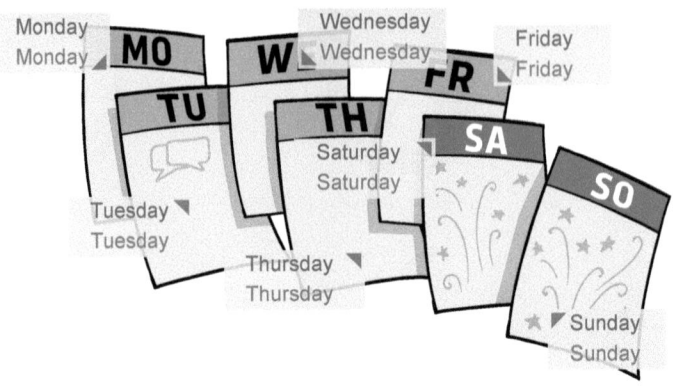

yesterday

yesterday

today

today

tomorrow

tomorrow

morning

morning

noon

noon

evening

evening

business days

workdays

weekend

weekend

year

year

rain
rain
spring
spring
summer
summer
wind
wind
autumn
fall
snow
snow
winter
winter

4.APRIL 11°
5.APRIL 4°
6.APRIL 13°
7.APRIL 8°
8.APRIL 10°

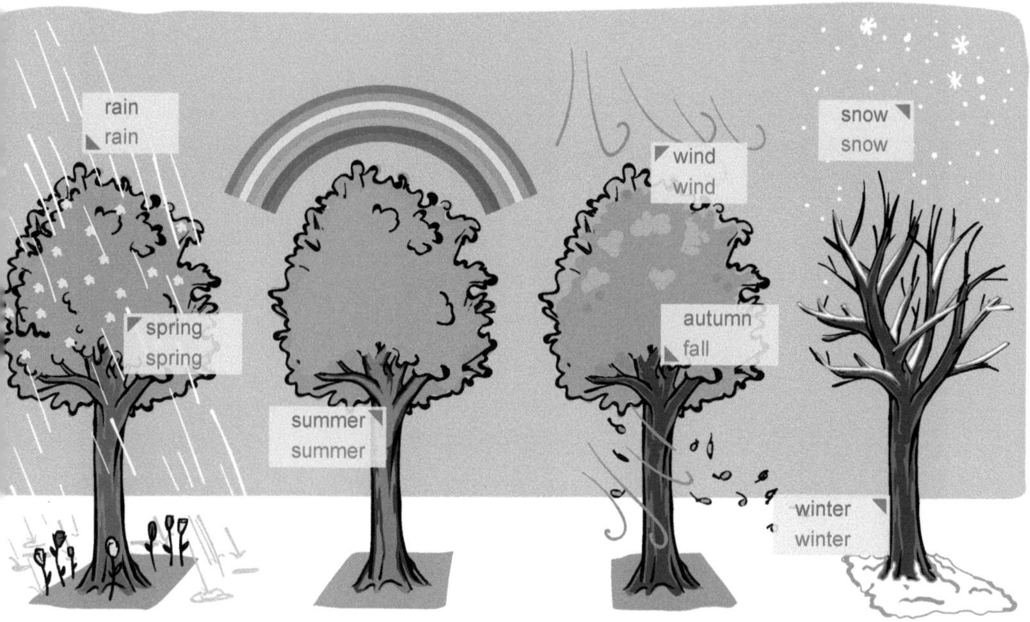

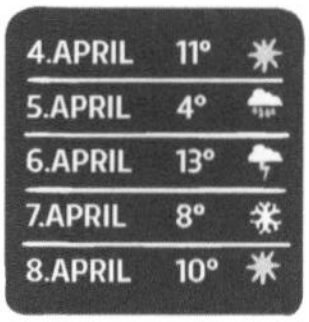

weather forecast

weather forecast

F
C
120
90
60
30
0
-30
40
30
20
10
0
-10
-20

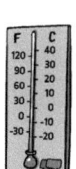

thermometer

thermometer

sunshine

sunshine

cloud

cloud

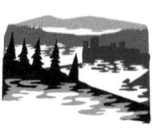

fog

fog

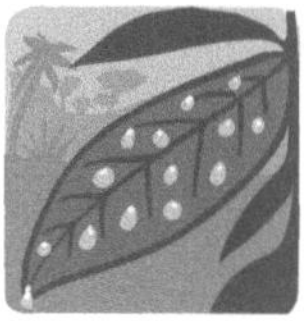

humidity

humidity

lightning

lightning

thunder

thunder

storm

storm

hail

hail

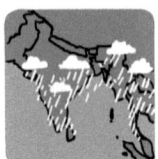

monsoon

monsoon

flood

flood

ice

ice

January

January

February

February

March

March

April

April

May

May

June

June

July

July

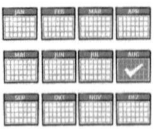

August

August

year - year

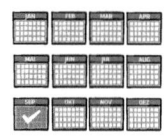

September
September

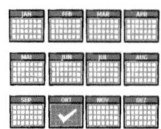

October
October

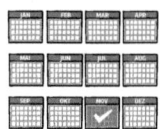

November
November

December
December

shapes
shapes

circle
circle

square
square

rectangle
rectangle

triangle
triangle

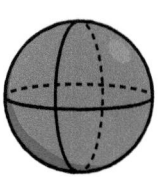

sphere
sphere

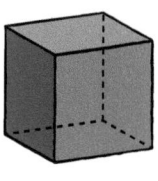

cube
cube

white

white

yellow

yellow

orange

orange

pink

pink

red

red

purple

purple

blue

blue

green

green

brown

brown

grey

gray

black

black

a lot / a little

a lot / a little

angry / calm

angry / calm

beautiful / ugly

beautiful / ugly

beginning / end

beginning / end

big / small

big / small

bright / dark

bright / dark

brother / sister

brother / sister

clean / dirty

clean / dirty

complete / incomplete

complete / incomplete

day / night

day / night

dead / alive

dead / alive

wide / narrow

wide / narrow

edible / inedible

edible / inedible

evil / kind

evil / kind

excited / bored

excited / bored

fat / thin

fat / thin

first / last

first / last

friend / enemy

friend / enemy

full / empty

full / empty

hard / soft

hard / soft

heavy / light

heavy / light

hunger / thirst

hunger / thirst

ill / healthy

ill / healthy

illegal / legal

illegal / legal

intelligent / stupid

intelligent / stupid

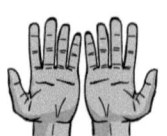

left / right

left / right

near / far

near / far

opposites - opposites

new / used

new / used

nothing / something

nothing / something

old / young

old / young

on / off

on / off

open / closed

open / closed

quiet / loud

quiet / loud

rich / poor

rich / poor

right / wrong

right / wrong

rough / smooth

rough / smooth

sad / happy

sad / happy

short / long

short / long

slow / fast

slow / fast

wet / dry

wet / dry

warm / cool

warm / cool

war / peace

war / peace

0

zero

zero

1

one

one

2

two

two

3

three

three

4

four

four

5

five

five

6

six

six

7

seven

seven

8

eight

eight

9

nine

nine

10

ten

ten

11

eleven

eleven

12

twelve

twelve

13

thirteen

thirteen

14

fourteen

fourteen

15

fifteen

fifteen

16

sixteen

sixteen

17

seventeen

seventeen

18

eighteen

eighteen

19

nineteen

nineteen

20

twenty

twenty

100

hundred

hundred

1.000

thousand

thousand

1.000.000

million

million

languages

English

English

American English

American English

Chinese Mandarin

Chinese Mandarin

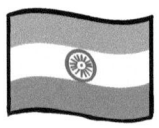

Hindi

Hindi

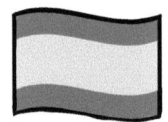

Spanish

Spanish

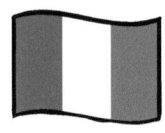

French

French

Arabic

Arabic

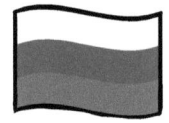

Russian

Russian

Portuguese

Portuguese

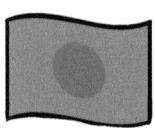

Bengali

Bengali

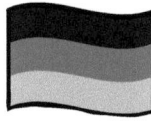

German

German

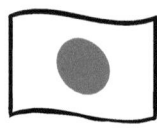

Japanese

Japanese

I
I

you
you

he / she / it
he / she / it

we
we

you
you

they
they

who?
who?

what?
what?

how?
how?

where?
where?

when?
when?

HELLO, I AM

name
name

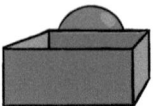

behind

behind

in

in

in front of

in front of

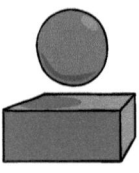

over

over

on

on

under

under

beside

beside

between

between

place

place